D1269573

GARY SNYDER

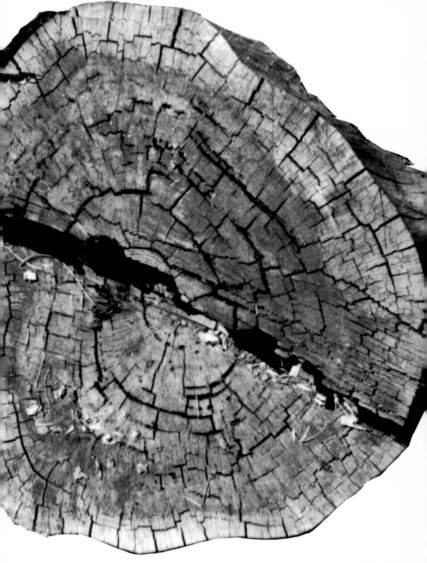

MYTHS & TEXTS

MYTHS & TEXTS

OTHER BOOKS BY GARY SNYDER

GARY SNYDER
MYTHS & TEXTS

A NEW DIRECTIONS BOOK

ACKNOWLEDGMENTS
Some of the poems in this book first appeared in *Ark, Black Mountain Review, Bussei, The Fifties, Galley Sail Review, Jabberwock, The Needle, Poems & Pictures,* and *Yugen.*

Myths & Texts was originally published in 1960 by Totem Press in association with Corinth Books and is reissued by special arrangement with the latter.

Manufactured in the United States of America
New Directions books are printed on acid-free paper
First published clothbound and as New Directions Paperbook 457 in 1978
Published simultaneously in Canada by Penguin Books Canada Limited

Library of Congress Cataloging in Publication Data

Snyder, Gary.
  Myths & texts.
  (A New Directions Book)
  I. Title.
PS3569.N88M9   1978   811'.5'4   77–25378
ISBN 0–8112–0685–8
ISBN 0–8112–0686–6 pbk.

New Directions Books are published for James Laughlin
by New Directions Publishing Corporation,
80 Eighth Avenue, New York 10011

SEVENTH PRINTING

FOR LLOYD REYNOLDS
AND DAVID FRENCH

So that not only this our craft
is in danger to be set at nought;
but also the temple of the great
Goddess Diana should be despised,
and her magnificence should be destroyed,
whom all Asia and the world worshippeth.

—Acts 19:27

INTRODUCTION

I set this poem loose in the world some years ago. It looks like an old friend I haven't seen a while, except, have I changed and has it stayed the same? But poems, like people, keep changing through time. In some ways this poem has changed for the better: it is clearer, more accessible now than when it first came through me.

North America, North Pacific, the Far East are more seen as connected; Chinese, Amerindian, Japanese lore is more translated. The references to gods, peoples, and places sound less exotic, which is right; the Buddha, Seami, the Great Bear are not exotica but part of our whole planetary heritage.

About *Myths and Texts* I once wrote (for Donald Allen): ". . . it grew between 1952 and 1956. Its several rhythms are based on long days of quiet in lookout cabins; setting chokers for the Warm Springs Lumber Co. (looping cables on logs and hooking them to D8 Caterpillars—dragging and rumbling through the brush); and the songs and dances of Great Basin Indian tribes I used to hang around. The title comes from the happy collections Sapir, Boas, Swanton, and others made of American Indian folktales early in this century; it also means the two sources of human knowledge—symbols and sense-impressions. I tried to make my life as a hobo and worker, the questions of history and philosophy in my head, and the glimpses of the roots of religion I'd seen through meditation, peyote, and 'secret frantic rituals' into one whole thing. As far as I'm concerned, I succeeded."

Succeeded, I meant, only for my own needs of the time, and not for anyone else. I guess it was prideful and wrong to say succeeded at all, for the work is far from finished. The effort of this kind of poetry remains one of our most challenging enterprises: here on Occupied Turtle Island, we are most of us a still rootless population of non-natives who don't even know the plants or where our water comes from. Myself, raised in the West, in the basin of Puget Sound, what some poets now call Ish Nation, set out like everyone else, to make sense, and to find somehow a way to actually "belong to the land."

I also wrote once: "As poet I hold the most archaic values on earth. They go back to the upper Palaeolithic: the fertility of the soil, the magic of animals, the power-vision in solitude, the terrifying initiation and rebirth, the love and ecstasy of the dance, the common work of the tribe."

Why this going back into the roots and the past, instead of leaping off into the future, I'm sometimes asked. But it's not *in time* at all that we study our world and ourselves. There's no close or far. We have, simply, the chance to fill out the whole picture now, for the first time in human experience. It is beginning to be possible to look in one wide gaze at all that human beings have been and done on the whole planet, as one small part of the web of Gaia the earth-life-Goddess.

Then turn that over and over in the depths of deepest symbol-holding store-house-consciousness mind, to maybe let another flower of clarity rise from the compost of information. Such flowers set us truly free and only come every few millennia. I'm glad *Myths & Texts* is a warm part of the compost in this end-of-the-century spectacle. I hope it helps toward growing that flower that will be totally in the present.

GS 13.X.40077

LOGGING

1

The morning star is not a star
Two seedling fir, one died
                    Io, Io,
Girdled in wistaria
Wound with ivy
                    "The May Queen
Is the survival of
A pre-human
Rutting season"

The year spins
Pleiades sing to their rest
                    at San Francisco
                    dream
                    dream
Green comes out of the ground
Birds squabble
Young girls run mad with the pine bough,
                                        Io

2

But ye shall destroy their altars,
    break their images, and cut down their groves.
                                —*Exodus 34:13*

The ancient forests of China logged
    and the hills slipped into the Yellow Sea.
Squared beams, log dogs,
    on a tamped-earth sill.

3

San Francisco 2×4s
    were the woods around Seattle:
Someone killed and someone built, a house,
    a forest, wrecked or raised
All America hung on a hook
    & burned by men, in their own praise.

Snow on fresh stumps and brush-piles.
The generator starts and rumbles
                in the frosty dawn
I wake from bitter dreams,
Rise and build a fire,
Pull on and lace the stiff cold boots
Eat huge flapjacks by a gloomy Swede
In splintery cookhouse light
                grab my tin pisspot hat
Ride off to the show in a crummy-truck
And start the Cat.

"Pines grasp the clouds with iron claws
like dragons rising from sleep"
250,000 board-feet a day
If both Cats keep working
& nobody gets hurt

3

"Lodgepole Pine: the wonderful reproductive
power of this species on areas over which its
stand has been killed by fire is dependent upon
the ability of the closed cones to endure a fire
which kills the tree without injuring its seed.
After fire, the cones open and shed their seeds
on the bared ground and a new growth springs up."

4

Stood straight
                    holding the choker high
As the Cat swung back the arch
                    piss-firs falling,
Limbs snapping on the tin hat
                    bright D caught on
Swinging butt-hooks
                    ringing against cold steel.

Hsü Fang lived on leeks and pumpkins.
Goosefoot,
            wild herbs,
                        fields lying fallow!

But it's hard to farm
Between the stumps:
The cows get thin, the milk tastes funny,
The kids grow up and go to college
They don't come back.
                    the little fir-trees do

            Rocks the same blue as sky
Only icefields, a mile up,
                        are the mountain
Hovering over ten thousand acres
Of young fir.

4

Pines, under pines,
       Seami Motokiyo
       The Doer stamps his foot.
       A thousand board-feet
Bucked, skidded, loaded—
(Takasago, Ise) float in a mill pond;
A thousand years dancing
Flies in the saw kerf.

Cliff by Tomales Bay
Seal's slick head
       head shoulders breasts
       glowing in night saltwater
Skitter of fish, and above, behind the pines,
Bear grunts, stalking the Pole-star.

Foot-whack on polished boards
Slide and stop; drum-thump.
"Today's wind moves in the pines"
             falling
And skidding the red-bark pine.
Clouds over Olallie Butte
Scatter rain on the Schoolie flat.
A small bear slips out the wet brush
          crosses the creek
Seami, Kwanami,
       Gone too.
Through the pines.

5

Again the ancient, meaningless
Abstractions of the educated mind.
       wet feet and the campfire out.
Drop a mouthful of useless words.
—The book's in the crapper
They're up to the part on Ethics now

       skidding logs in pine-flat heat
       long summer sun
       the flax bag sweet
Summer professors
       elsewhere meet
Indiana? Seattle? Ann Arbor?
       bug clack in sage
Sudden rumble of wheels on cattle-guard rails.
       hitching & hiking
       looking for work.

"We rule you" all crownéd or be-Homburged heads
"We fool you" those guys with Ph.D.s
"We eat for you" you
"We work for you" who?
     a big picture of K. Marx with an axe,
"Where I cut off one it will never grow again."
     O Karl would it were true
     I'd put my saw to work for you
& the wicked social tree would fall right down.

(The only logging we'll do here is trees
And do it quick, with big trucks and machines)
     "That Cat wobbles like a sick whore"
So we lay on our backs tinkering
              all afternoon
The trees and the logs stood still
It was so quiet we could hear the birds.

6

"In that year, 1914, we lived on the farm
And the relatives lived with us.
A banner year for wild blackberries
Dad was crazy about wild blackberries
No berries like that now.
You know Kitsap County was logged before
The turn of the century—it was easiest of all,
Close to water, virgin timber,
When I was a kid walking about in the
Stumpland, wherever you'd go a skidroad
Puncheon, all overgrown.
We went up one like that, fighting our way through
To its end near the top of a hill:
For some reason wild blackberries
Grew best there. We took off one morning
Right after milking: rode the horses
To a valley we'd been to once before
Hunting berries, and hitched the horses.
About a quarter mile up the old road
We found the full ripe of berrytime—
And with only two pails—so we
Went back home, got Mother and Ruth,
And filled lots of pails. Mother sent letters
To all the relatives in Seattle:
Effie, Aunt Lucy, Bill Moore,
Forrest, Edna, six or eight, they all came
Out to the farm, and we didn't take pails
Then: we took copper clothes-boilers,
Wash-tubs, buckets, and all went picking.
We were canning for three days."

Felix Baran
Hugo Gerlot
Gustav Johnson
John Looney
Abraham Rabinowitz
Shot down on the steamer Verona
For the shingle-weavers of Everett
   the Everett Massacre November 5 1916

Ed McCullough, a logger for thirty-five years
Reduced by the advent of chainsaws
To chopping off knots at the landing:
"I don't have to take this kind of shit,
Another twenty years
  and I'll tell 'em to shove it"
  (he was sixty-five then)
In 1934 they lived in shanties
At Hooverville, Sullivan's Gulch.
When the Portland-bound train came through
The trainmen tossed off coal.

"Thousands of boys shot and beat up
For wanting a good bed, good pay,
   decent food, in the woods—"
No one knew what it meant:
"Soldiers of Discontent."

8

Each dawn is clear
Cold air bites the throat.
Thick frost on the pine bough
Leaps from the tree
     snapped by the diesel

Drifts and glitters in the
      horizontal sun.
In the frozen grass
      smoking boulders
      ground by steel tracks.
In the frozen grass
      wild horses stand
      beyond a row of pines.
The D8 tears through piss-fir,
Scrapes the seed-pine
         chipmunks flee,
A black ant carries an egg
Aimlessly from the battered ground.
Yellowjackets swarm and circle
Above the crushed dead log, their home.
Pitch oozes from barked
      trees still standing,
Mashed bushes make strange smells.
Lodgepole pines are brittle.
Camprobbers flutter to watch.

A few stumps, drying piles of brush;
Under the thin duff, a toe-scrape down
Black lava of a late flow.
Leaves stripped from thornapple
Taurus by nightfall.

9

Headed home, hitch-hiking
leaving mountains behind
where all Friday in sunlight
fighting flies fixed phone line
high on the lake trail,
dreaming of home,
by night to my girl and a late bath.
she came in naked to the tub
her breasts hung glistening
and she scrubbed my back.
we made love night-long.
she was unhappy alone.
all Sunday softly talked,
I left, two hundred miles
hitching back to work.

10

A ghost logger wanders a shadow
In the early evening, boots squeak
With the cicada, the fleas
Nest warm in his blanket-roll
Berrybrambles catch at the stagged pants
He stumbles up the rotted puncheon road
There is a logging camp
Somewhere in there among the alders
Berries and high rotting stumps
Bindlestiff with a wooden bowl
(The poor bastards at Nemi in the same boat)
What old Seattle skidroad did he walk from
Fifty years too late, and all his
                    money spent?

Dogfish and Shark oil
Greasing the skids.
"Man is the heart of the universe
the upshot of the five elements,
born to enjoy food and color and noise . . ."
Get off my back Confucius
There's enough noise now.
What bothers me is all those stumps:
What did they do with the wood?
Them Xtians out to save souls and grab land
"They'd steal Christ off the cross
                    if he wasn't nailed on"
The last decent carpentry
Ever done by Jews.

11

Ray Wells, a big Nisqually, and I
              each set a choker
On the butt-logs of two big Larch
In a thornapple thicket and a swamp.
              waiting for the Cat to come back,
"Yesterday we gelded some ponies
"My father-in-law cut the skin on the balls
"He's a Wasco and don't speak English
"He grabs a handful of tubes and somehow
              cuts the right ones.
"The ball jumps out, the horse screams
"But he's all tied up.
The Caterpillar clanked back down.
In the shadow of that racket
              diesel and iron tread
I thought of Ray Wells' tipi out on the sage flat
The gelded ponies
Healing and grazing in the dead white heat.

12

A green limb hangs in the crotch
Of a silver snag,
Above the Cats,
            the skidders and thudding brush,
Hundreds of butterflies
Flit through the pines.
"You shall live in square
            gray houses in a barren land
            and beside those square gray
            houses you shall starve."
—Drinkswater. Who saw a vision
At the high and lonely center of the earth:
Where Crazy Horse
            went to watch the Morning Star,
& the four-legged people, the creeping people,
The standing people and the flying people
Know how to talk.
I ought to have eaten
Whale tongue with them.
            they keep saying I used to be a human being
"He-at-whose-voice-the-Ravens-sit-on-the-sea."
Sea-foam washing the limpets and barnacles
Rattling the gravel beach
Salmon up creek, bear on the bank,
Wild ducks over the mountains weaving
In a long south flight, the land of
Sea and fir tree with the pine-dry
Sage-flat country to the east.
Han Shan could have lived here,
            & no scissorbill stooge of the
            Emperor would have come trying to steal
            his last poor shred of sense.

On the wooded coast, eating oysters
Looking off toward China and Japan
"If you're gonna work these woods
Don't want nothing
That can't be left out in the rain—"

13

T 36N   R 16E   S 25
Is burning. Far to the west.
A north creek side,
          flame to the crowns
Sweeping a hillside bare—
          in another district,
On a different drainage.

Smoke higher than clouds
Turning the late sun red.

Cumulus, blowing north
          high cirrus
Drifting east,
          smoke
Filling the west.

The crews have departed,
And I am not concerned.

The groves are down
               cut down
Groves of Ahab, of Cybele
Pine trees, knobbed twigs
     thick cone and seed
     Cybele's tree this, sacred in groves
Pine of Seami, cedar of Haida
Cut down by the prophets of Israel
     the fairies of Athens
     the thugs of Rome
               both ancient and modern;
Cut down to make room for the suburbs
Bulldozed by Luther and Weyerhaeuser
Crosscut and chainsaw
     squareheads and finns
     high-lead and cat-skidding
Trees down
Creeks choked, trout killed, roads.

Sawmill temples of Jehovah.
Squat black burners 100 feet high
Sending the smoke of our burnt
Live sap and leaf
To his eager nose.

Lodgepole
        cone/seed waits for fire
And then thin forests of silver-gray.
        in the void
        a pine cone falls
Pursued by squirrels
What mad pursuit! What struggle to escape!

Her body a seedpod
Open to the wind
"A seed pod void of seed
We had no meeting together"
        so you and I must wait
Until the next blaze
Of the world, the universe,
Millions of worlds, burning
        —oh let it lie.

Shiva at the end of the kalpa:
Rock-fat, hill-flesh, gone in a whiff.
Men who hire men to cut groves
Kill snakes, build cities, pave fields,
Believe in god, but can't
Believe their own senses
Let alone Gautama. Let them lie.

Pine sleeps, cedar splits straight
Flowers crack the pavement.
        Pa-ta Shan-jen
(A painter who watched Ming fall)
        lived in a tree:
"The brush
May paint the mountains and streams
Though the territory is lost."

HUNTING

1

first shaman song

In the village of the dead,
Kicked loose bones
         ate pitch of a drift log
         (whale fat)
Nettles and cottonwood. Grass smokes
                    in the sun
Logs turn in the river
         sand scorches the feet.

Two days without food, trucks roll past
         in dust and light, rivers
         are rising.
Thaw in the high meadows. Move west in July.

Soft oysters rot now, between tides
         the flats stink.

I sit without thoughts by the log-road
Hatching a new myth
watching the waterdogs
         the last truck gone.

2

Atok: creeping
Maupok: waiting
    to hunt seals.

The sea hunter
     watching the whirling seabirds on the rocks
The mountain hunter
     horn-tipped shaft on a snowslope
     edging across cliffs for a shot at goat
"Upon the lower slopes of the mountain,
on the cover, we find the sculptured forms
of animals apparently lying dead in the
wilderness" thus Fenellosa
On the pottery of Shang.

It's a shame I didn't kill you,
          Yang Kuei Fei,
Cut down in the old apartment
Left to bleed between the bookcase and the wall,
I'd hunt you still, trail you from town to town.
But you change shape.
         death's a new shape,
Maybe flayed you'd be true
But it wouldn't be through.

"You who live with your grandmother
I'll trail you with dogs
And crush you in my mouth."
        —not that we're cruel—
But a man's got to eat

3

this poem is for birds

Birds in a whirl, drift to the rooftops
Kite dip, swing to the seabank fogroll
Form: dots in air changing line from line,
        the future defined.

Brush back smoke from the eyes,
                    dust from the mind,
With the wing-feather fan of an eagle.
A hawk drifts into the far sky.
A marmot whistles across huge rocks.
Rain on the California hills.
Mussels clamp to sea-boulders
Sucking the Spring tides

Rain soaks the tan stubble
Fields full of ducks

Rain sweeps the Eucalyptus
Strange pines on the coast
                    needles two to the bunch
The whole sky whips in the wind
Vaux Swifts
Flying before the storm
Arcing close hear sharp wing-whistle
Sickle-bird
                pale gray
                sheets of rain slowly shifting
                down from the clouds,
Black Swifts.
                —the swifts cry
As they shoot by, See or go blind!

4

The swallow-shell that eases birth
    brought from the south by Hummingbird.
"We pull out the seagrass, the seagrass,
    the seagrass, and it drifts away"
—song of the geese.

"My children
    their father was a log"
—song of the pheasant.
The white gulls south of Victoria
    catch tossed crumbs in midair.
When anyone hears the Catbird
    he gets lonesome.
San Francisco, "Mulberry Harbor"
    eating the speckled sea-bird eggs
    of the Farallones.
Driving sand sends swallows flying,
        warm mud puts the ducks to sleep.
Magical birds: Phoenix, hawk, and crane
        owl and gander, wren,
Bright eyes aglow: Polishing clawfoot
        with talons spread, subtle birds
Wheel and go, leaving air in shreds
        black beaks shine in gray haze.
Brushed by the hawk's wing
    of vision.

—They were arguing about the noise
Made by the Golden-eye Duck.
Some said the whistling sound
Was made by its nose, some said
No, by the wings.
        "Have it your way.
We will leave you forever."
They went upriver:
The Flathead tribe.

        Raven
    on a roost of furs
No bird in a bird-book,
        black as the sun.

5

the making of the horn spoon

The head of the mountain-goat is in the corner
      for the making of the horn spoon,
The black spoon. When fire's heat strikes it
      turn the head
Four days and hair pulls loose
      horn twists free.
Hand-adze, straightknife, notch the horn-base;
      rub with rough sandstone
Shave down smooth. Split two cedar sticks
      when water boils plunge the horn,
Tie mouth between sticks in the spoon shape
      rub with dried dogfish skin.
It will be black and smooth,
      a spoon.

Wa, laEm gwała ts!ololaqe ka · ts!Enaqe laxeq.

6

this poem is for bear

"As for me I am a child of the god of the mountains."

A bear down under the cliff.
She is eating huckleberries.
They are ripe now
Soon it will snow, and she
Or maybe he, will crawl into a hole
And sleep. You can see

23

Huckleberries in bearshit if you
Look, this time of year
If I sneak up on the bear
It will grunt and run

The others had all gone down
From the blackberry brambles, but one girl
Spilled her basket, and was picking up her
Berries in the dark.
A tall man stood in the shadow, took her arm,
Led her to his home. He was a bear.
In a house under the mountain
She gave birth to slick dark children
With sharp teeth, and lived in the hollow
Mountain many years.
                    snare a bear: call him out:
honey-eater
forest apple
light-foot
Old man in the fur coat, Bear! come out!
Die of your own choice!
Grandfather black-food!
                    this girl married a bear
Who rules in the mountains, Bear!
                        you have eaten many berries
                        you have caught many fish
                        you have frightened many people

Twelve species north of Mexico
Sucking their paws in the long winter
Tearing the high-strung caches down
Whining, crying, jacking off
(Odysseus was a bear)

Bear-cubs gnawing the soft tits
Teeth gritted, eyes screwed tight
                    but she let them.

Til her brothers found the place
Chased her husband up the gorge
Cornered him in the rocks.
Song of the snared bear:
      "Give me my belt.
      "I am near death.
      "I came from the mountain caves
      "At the headwaters,
      "The small streams there
      "Are all dried up.

—I think I'll go hunt bears.
            "hunt bears?
Why shit Snyder,
You couldn't hit a bear in the ass
      with a handful of rice!"

7

All beaded with dew
      dawn grass runway
Open-eyed rabbits hang
      dangle, loose feet in tall grass
From alder snares.
The spider is building a morning-web
From the snared rabbit's ear to the snare

      down trail at sunrise
      wet berry brush
      spiderwebs in the eyes
Gray chunk rocks roll down
Splinter pines,
      bark the firs,
          rest in maple shade.

I dance
On every swamp
           sang the rabbit
    once a hungry ghost
    then a beast
    who knows what next?

Salmon, deer, no pottery;
Summer and winter houses
Roots, berries, watertight baskets—
Our girls get layed by Coyote
We get along
           just fine.
The Shuswap tribe.

8

this poem is for deer

"I dance on all the mountains
On five mountains, I have a dancing place
When they shoot at me I run
To my five mountains"

Missed a last shot
At the Buck, in twilight
So we came back sliding
On dry needles through cold pines.
Scared out a cottontail
Whipped up the winchester
Shot off its head.
The white body rolls and twitches
In the dark ravine
As we run down the hill to the car.
              deer foot down scree

Picasso's fawn, Issa's fawn,
Deer on the autumn mountain
Howling like a wise man
Stiff springy jumps down the snowfields
Head held back, forefeet out,
Balls tight in a tough hair sack
Keeping the human soul from care
                    on the autumn mountain
Standing in late sun, ear-flick
Tail-flick, gold mist of flies
Whirling from nostril to eyes.

.   .   .

Home by night
                drunken eye
Still picks out Taurus
Low, and growing high:
                four-point buck
Dancing in the headlights
                on the lonely road
A mile past the mill-pond,
With the car stopped, shot
That wild silly blinded creature down.

Pull out the hot guts
                with hard bare hands
While night-frost chills the tongue
                and eye
The cold horn-bones.
The hunter's belt
                just below the sky
Warm blood in the car trunk.
Deer-smell,
                the limp tongue.

.   .   .

Deer don't want to die for me.
                    I'll drink sea-water
Sleep on beach pebbles in the rain
Until the deer come down to die
                    in pity for my pain.

9

Sealion, salmon, offshore—
Salt-fuck desire driving flap fins
North, south, five thousand miles
Coast, and up creek, big seeds
Groping for inland womb.

Geese, ducks, swallows,
                    paths in the air
I am a frozen addled egg on the tundra

My petrel, snow-tongued
                    kiss her a brook her mouth
of smooth pebbles her tongue a bed
                    icewater flowing in that
Cavern dark, tongue drifts in the creek
                    —blind fish

On the rainy boulders
On the bloody sandbar
I ate the spawned-out salmon
I went crazy
Covered with ashes
Gnawing the girls breasts
Marrying women to whales
Or dogs, I'm a priest too
I raped your wife
I'll eat your corpse

10

Flung from demonic wombs
        off to some new birth
A million shapes—just look in any
        biology book.
And the hells below mind
        where ghosts roam, the heavens
Above brain, where gods & angels play
        an age or two
& they'll trade with you,
Who wants heaven?
        rest homes like that
Scattered all through the galaxy.

     "I kill everything
     I fear nothing but wolves
     From the mouth of the Cowlitz
             to its source,
     Only the wolves scare me,
     I have a chief's tail"
—Skunk.
     "We carry deer-fawns in our mouths
     We carry deer-fawns in our mouths
     We have our faces blackened"
—Wolf-song.
"If I were a baby seal
             every time I came up
I'd head toward shore—"

11

songs for a four-crowned dancing hat

O Prajapati
            You who floated on the sea
            Hatched to godhead in the slime
Heated red and beaten for a bronze ritual bowl
The Boar!
            Dripping boar emerged
            On his tusk his treasure
Prajapati from the sea-depths:
Skewered body of the earth
Each time I carry you this way.

The year I wore my Raven skin
    Dogfish ran. Too many berries on the hill
Grizzly fat and happy in the sun—
    The little women, the fern women,
They have stopped crying now.
    "What will you do with human beings?
Are you going to save the human beings?"
    That was Southeast, they say.

12

Out the Greywolf valley
in late afternoon
after eight days in the high meadows
hungry, and out of food,
the trail broke into a choked
clearing, apples grew gone wild
hung on one low bough by a hornet's nest.

30

caught the drone in tall clover
lowland smell in the shadows
then picked a hard green one:
watched them swarm.
smell of the mountains still on me.
none stung.

13

Now I'll also tell what food
we lived on then:

Mescal, yucca fruit, pinyon, acorns,
prickly pear, sumac berry, cactus,
spurge, dropseed, lip fern, corn,
mountain plants, wild potatoes, mesquite,
stems of yucca, tree-yucca flowers, chokecherries,
pitahaya cactus, honey of the ground-bee,
honey, honey of the bumblebee,
mulberries, angle-pod, salt, berries,
berries of the one-seeded juniper,
berries of the alligator-bark juniper,
wild cattle, mule deer, antelopes,
white-tailed deer, wild turkeys, doves, quail,
squirrels, robins, slate-colored juncoes,
song sparrows, wood rats, prairie dogs,
rabbits, peccaries, burros, mules, horses,
buffaloes, mountain sheep, and turtles.

14

Buddha fed himself to tigers
& donated mountains of eyes
          (through the years)
To the blind,
               a mountain-lion
Once trailed me four miles
At night and no gun
It was awful, I didn't want to be ate
          maybe we'll change.

Or make a net of your sister's cunt-hair
Catch the sun, and burn the world.

Where are you going now?
Shake hands.
Goodbye, George Bell . . .
               that was a Kwakiutl woman
               singing goodbye to her man,
               Victoria B.C., 1887

The mules are loaded
               packs lashed with a vajra-hitch
               the grass-eaters steam in the dawn
               the workers are still asleep
               light swings on the high cornice
               on the chill side of the mountain, we
               switchback
               drink at the waterfall
               start to climb
"Stalk lotuses
Burst through the rocks
And come up in sevens."

15

First day of the world.
White rock ridges
                new born
Jay chatters   the first time
Rolling a smoke by the campfire
New! never before.
                bitter coffee, cold
Dawn wind, sun on the cliffs,
You'll find it in *Many old shoes*
High!   high on poetry & mountains.

That silly ascetic Gautama
         thought he knew something;
Maudgalyâyana   knew hell
Knew every hell, from the
Cambrian to the Jurassic
He suffered in them all.

16

How rare to be born a human being!
Wash him off with cedar-bark and milkweed
         send the damned doctors home.
Baby, baby, noble baby
Noble-hearted baby

One hand up, one hand down
"I alone am the honored one"
Birth of the Buddha.
And the whole world-system trembled.
"If that baby really said that,
I'd cut him up and throw him to the dogs!"

said Chao-chou the Zen Master. But
Chipmunks, gray squirrels, and
Golden-mantled ground squirrels
                brought him each a nut.
Truth being the sweetest of flavors.

Girls would have in their arms
A wild gazelle or wild wolf-cubs
And give them their white milk,
                those who had new-born infants home
Breasts still full.
Wearing a spotted fawnskin
                sleeping under trees
                bacchantes, drunk
On wine or truth, what you will,
Meaning: compassion.
Agents: man and beast, beasts
Got the buddha-nature
All but
Coyote.

BURNING

1

second shaman song

Squat in swamp shadows.
      mosquitoes sting;
        high light in cedar above.
Crouched in a dry vain frame
     —thirst for cold snow
     —green slime of bone marrow
Seawater fills each eye

Quivering in nerve and muscle
Hung in the pelvic cradle
Bones propped against roots
A blind flicker of nerve

Still hand moves out alone
Flowering and leafing
         turning to quartz
Streaked rock   congestion of karma
The long body of the swamp.
A mud-streaked thigh.

Dying carp biting air
       in the damp grass,
River recedes. No matter.

Limp fish sleep in the weeds
The sun dries me as I dance

2

One moves continually with the consciousness
Of that other, totally alien, non-human:
Humming inside like a taut drum,
Carefully avoiding any direct thought of it,
Attentive to the real-world flesh and stone.

Intricate layers of emptiness
This only world, juggling forms
            a hand, a breast, two clasped
Human tenderness scuttles
Down dry endless cycles
Forms within forms falling
                        clinging
Loosely, what's gone away?
                    —love

In Spring the Avocado sheds dead leaves
Soft rattling through the Cherry greens
Bird at this moment
All these books
    wearing a thin sweater
    & no brassiere
    in failing light
One glance, miles below
Bones & flesh knit in the rock
    "have no regret—
chip chip
        (sparrows)
& not a word about the void
To which one hand diddling
Cling

3

Maudgalyâyana saw hell

Under the shuddering eyelid
Dreams gnawing the nerve-strings,
The mind grabs and the shut eye sees:
Down dimensions floating below sunlight,
Worlds of the dead, Bardo, mind-worlds
& horror of sunless cave-ritual
Meeting conscious monk bums
Blown on winds of karma from hell
To endless changing hell,
Life and death whipped
On this froth of reality (wind & rain
Realms human and full of desire) over the cold
Hanging enormous unknown, below
Art and History and all mankind living thoughts,
Occult & witchcraft evils each all true.
The thin edge of nature rising fragile
And helpless with its love and sentient stone
And flesh, above dark drug-death dreams.

Clouds I cannot lose, we cannot leave.
We learn to love, horror accepted.
Beyond, within, all normal beauties
Of the science-conscious sex and love-receiving
Day-to-day got vision of this sick
Sparkling person at the inturned dreaming
Blooming human mind
Dropping it all, and opening the eyes.

4

Maitreya the future Buddha

He's out stuck in a bird's craw
                              last night
Wildcat vomited his pattern on the snow.

Who refused to learn to dance, refused
To kiss you long ago. You fed him berries
But fled, the red stain on his teeth;
And when he cried, finding the world a Wheel—
              you only stole his rice,
Being so small and gray. He will not go,
But wait through fish scale, shale dust, bone
              of hawk and marmot,
              caught leaves in ice,
Til flung on a new net of atoms:
Snagged in flight
Leave you hang and quiver like a gong

Your empty happy body
Swarming in the light

5

jimson weed

Now both
Being persons—alive
We sit here
The wind
Whirls
        "Don't kill it man,

The roach is the best part"
      still an incessant chatter
On Vulture Peak
Crack of dawn/   calor/canor/dulcor   faugh

I hold it
I tell of it, standing
I look here
I look there
Standing
      great limp mouth
      hanging loose in air
      quivers, turns in upon itself,
      gone
      with a diabolical laugh
The night bat
Rising flies, I tell it
I sing it

"Jesus was a great doctor, I guess he was
the best gambler in the United States"
At Hakwinyava
Imagine a dark house
Blue

6

My clutch and your clutch
      batter the same bough
Elliptical, bird-light
      stink of spilled wine.
Whirling hills, lost out of mind.

When Red Hand came to the river he saw
a man sitting on the other side of the river
pointing with his arm. So Red Hand
sat and pointed with his arm until nightfall
when he suddenly realized that it was
only a dead tree with a stretched out limb
and he got up and crossed the river.

March wind
  blows the bright dawn
  apricot blossoms down.
  salty bacon smoking on the stove
  (sitting on Chao-chou's *wu*
      my feet sleep)

Ananda, grieving all night in the square
   gave up & went to bed & just then woke
The big trucks go by in the half-asleep night,
Ah, butterflies
Granite rots and crumbles
Warm seas & simple life slops on the ranges
Mayflies glitter for a day
Like Popes!

    where the sword is kept sharp
    the VOID
    gnashes its teeth

7

Face in the crook of her neck
    felt throb of vein
Smooth skin, her cool breasts
All naked in the dawn

                    "byrdes
sing forth from every bough"
                    where are they now
And dreamt I saw the Duke of Chou

The Mother whose body is the Universe
Whose breasts are Sun and Moon,
                    the statue of Prajna
From Java: the quiet smile,
The naked breasts.

"Will you still love me when my
        breasts get big?"
the little girl said—

"Earthly Mothers and those who suck
the breasts of earthly mothers are mortal—
but deathless are those who have fed
at the breast of the Mother of the Universe."

8

John Muir on Mt. Ritter:

After scanning its face again and again,
I began to scale it, picking my holds
With intense caution. About half-way
To the top, I was suddenly brought to
A dead stop, with arms outspread
Clinging close to the face of the rock
Unable to move hand or foot
Either up or down. My doom
Appeared fixed. I MUST fall.

There would be a moment of
Bewilderment, and then,
A lifeless rumble down the cliff
To the glacier below.
My mind seemed to fill with a
Stifling smoke. This terrible eclipse
Lasted only a moment, when life blazed
Forth again with preternatural clearness.
I seemed suddenly to become possessed
Of a new sense. My trembling muscles
Became firm again, every rift and flaw in
The rock was seen as through a microscope,
My limbs moved with a positiveness and precision
With which I seemed to have
Nothing at all to do.

9

Night here,   a covert
All spun, webs in one
                how without grabbing hold it?
—Get into the bird-cage
                without starting them singing.

"Forming the New Society
                Within the shell of the Old"
The motto in the Wobbly Hall
Some old Finns and Swedes playing cards
Fourth and Yesler in Seattle.
O you modest, retiring, virtuous young ladies
                pick the watercress, pluck the yarrow
"Kwan kwan" goes the crane in the field,
                I'll meet you tomorrow;
A million workers dressed in black and buried,
We make love in leafy shade.

Bodhidharma sailing the Yangtze on a reed
Lenin in a sealed train through Germany
Hsüan Tsang, crossing the Pamirs
Joseph, Crazy Horse, living the last free
      starving high-country winter of their tribes.
Surrender into freedom, revolt into slavery—
Confucius no better—
      (with Lao-tzu to keep him in check)
"Walking about the countryside
          all one fall
To a heart's content beating on stumps."

10

Amitabha's vow

"If, after obtaining Buddhahood, anyone in my land
    gets tossed in jail on a vagrancy rap, may I
    not attain highest perfect enlightenment.

    wild geese in the orchard
    frost on the new grass

"If, after obtaining Buddhahood, anyone in my land
    loses a finger coupling boxcars, may I
    not attain highest perfect enlightenment.

    mare's eye flutters
    jerked by the lead-rope
    stone-bright shoes flick back
    ankles trembling: down steep rock

"If, after obtaining Buddhahood, anyone in my land
    can't get a ride hitch-hiking all directions, may I
    not attain highest perfect enlightenment.

wet rocks buzzing
rain and thunder southwest
hair, beard, tingle
wind whips bare legs
we should go back
we don't

11

      Floating of vapor from brazier
Who hold emptiness
Whose bundle is broken, blank spot in creation
      still gong in a long-empty hall
            perceptions at idle play

  Q. What is the way of non-activity?
  A. It is activity
Ingather limbs, tighten the fingers
Press tongue to the roof
Roll the eyes
      dried & salted in the sun
In the dry, hard chrysalis, a pure bug waits hatching
Sudden flares: rush of water and bone
Netted, fitted
Flicker of action, nerves burnt in patterns
      fields of cabbages
      yet to consume
Imprint of flexible mouth-sounds,
Seared in the mind, on things.

Coyote: "I guess there never was a world anywhere"
Earthmaker: "I think if we find a little world,
      "I can fix it up."

46

12

I have terrible meditations
On the cells all water
            frail bodies
Moisting in a quiver;
Flares of life that settle
Into stone,
The hollow quaking of the soft parts
Over bone

The city of the Gandharvas,
            not a real city,
Only the memory of a city
Preserved in seed from beginningless time.
            a city crowded with books,
Thick grass on the streets,
            a race of dark people
Wearing thin sandals, reading all morning in alleys
Glazing black pots at night.

            the royal feast—
One man singing
Three join the chorus
            fifty-stringed *seh*
   red strings in the sound-board
      black wine
      raw fish
      plain soup
"Herrick thou art too coorse to love"
Hoarse cry of nighthawk
Circling & swooping in the still, bright dawn.

13

Spikes of new smell driven up nostrils
Expanding & deepening, ear-muscles
Straining and grasping the sounds
Mouth filled with bright fluid coldness
Tongue crushed by the weight of its flavors
      —the Nootka sold out for lemon drops
(What's this talk about not understanding!
     you're just a person who refuses to see.)

Poetry a riprap on the slick rock of metaphysics
"Put a Spanish halter on that whore of a mare
& I'll lead the bitch up any trail"

(how gentle! He should have whipped her first)

    the wind turns.
    a cold rain blows over the shale
    we sleep in the belly of a cloud.
(you think sex art and travel are enough?
         you're a skinful of cowdung)

South of the Yellow River the Emperor Wu
Set the army horses free in the mountain pastures,
Set the Buffalo free on the Plain of the Peach Grove.
Chariots and armor were smeared with blood
       and put away. They locked up
       the Arrows bag.
Smell of crushed spruce and burned snag-wood.
       remains of men,
Bone-chopped foul remains, thick stew
Food for crows—
       (blind, deaf, and dumb!
       shall we give him another chance?)

At Nyahaim-kuvara
Night has gone
Traveling to my land
        —that's a Mohave night
Our night too, you think brotherhood
Humanity & good intentions will stop it?
As long as you hesitate, no place to go.

Bluejay, out at the world's end
        perched, looked, & dashed
Through the crashing: his head is squashed.
        symplegades, the *mumonkwan,*
It's all vagina dentata
        (Jump!)
"Leap through an Eagle's snapping beak"

Actaeon saw Dhyana in the Spring.

        it was nothing special,
    misty rain on Mt. Baker,
        Neah Bay at low tide.

14

A skin-bound bundle of clutchings
        unborn and with no place to go
Balanced on the boundless compassion
Of diatoms, lava, and chipmunks.

Love, let it be,
Is a sacrifice
        knees, the cornered eyes
Tea on a primus stove after a cold swim

49

Intricate doors and clocks, the clothes
          we stand in—
Gaps between seedings, the right year,
Green shoots in the marshes
Creeks in the proper directions
Hills in proportion,
Astrologers, go-betweens present,
               a marriage has been.

Walked all day through live oak and manzanita,
Scrabbling through dust down Tamalpais—
Thought of high mountains;
Looked out on a sea of fog.
Two of us, carrying packs.

15

Stone-flake and salmon.
The pure, sweet, straight-splitting
               with a ping
Red cedar of the thick coast valleys
Shake-blanks on the mashed ferns
               the charred logs
Fireweed and bees
An old burn, by new alder
Creek on smooth stones,
Back there a Tarheel logger farm.
(High country fir still hunched in snow)

From Siwash strawberry-pickers in the Skagit
Down to the boys at Sac,
Living by the river
          riding flatcars to Fresno,

Across the whole country
Steep towns, flat towns, even New York,
And oceans and Europe & libraries & galleries
And the factories they make rubbers in
This whole spinning show
            (among others)
Watched by the Mt. Sumeru L.O.

From the middle of the universe
& them with no radio.
"What is imperfect is best"
            silver scum on the trout's belly
            rubs off on your hand.
It's all falling or burning—
            rattle of boulders
            steady dribbling of rocks down cliffs
            bark chips in creeks
Porcupine chawed here—
                        Smoke
From Tillamook a thousand miles
Soot and hot ashes. Forest fires.
Upper Skagit burned I think 1919
Smoke covered all northern Washington.
            lightning strikes, flares,
Blossoms a fire on the hill.
Smoke like clouds. Blotting the sun
Stinging the eyes.
The hot seeds steam underground
            still alive.

16

"Wash me on home, mama"
　　　　　　—song of the Kelp.
A chief's wife
Sat with her back to the sun
On the sandy beach, shredding cedar-bark.
Her fingers were slender
She didn't eat much.

"Get foggy
We're going out to dig
Buttercup roots"

Dream, Dream,
Earth! those beings living on your surface
none of them disappearing, will all be transformed.
When I have spoken to them
when they have spoken to me, from that moment on,
their words and their bodies which they
usually use to move about with, will all change.
I will not have heard them. Signed,
　　　　　　　(　　　)
　　　　　　　Coyote

17

the text

Sourdough mountain called a fire in:
Up Thunder Creek, high on a ridge.
Hiked eighteen hours, finally found
A snag and a hundred feet around on fire:
All afternoon and into night
Digging the fire line
Falling the burning snag
It fanned sparks down like shooting stars
Over the dry woods, starting spot-fires
Flaring in wind up Skagit valley
From the Sound.
Toward morning it rained.
We slept in mud and ashes,
Woke at dawn, the fire was out,
The sky was clear, we saw
The last glimmer of the morning star.

the myth

Fire up Thunder Creek and the mountain—
            troy's burning!
The cloud mutters
The mountains are your mind.
The woods bristle there,
Dogs barking and children shrieking
Rise from below.

Rain falls for centuries
Soaking the loose rocks in space
Sweet rain, the fire's out
The black snag glistens in the rain
& the last wisp of smoke floats up
Into the absolute cold
Into the spiral whorls of fire
The storms of the Milky Way
"Buddha incense in an empty world"
Black pit cold and light-year
Flame tongue of the dragon
Licks the sun

The sun is but a morning star

Crater Mt. L.O. 1952-Marin-an 1956

end of myths & texts

w Directions Paperbooks—A Partial Listing

r a complete listing request free catalog from
w Directions, 80 Eighth Avenue, New York 10011   †**Bilingual**

For a complete listing request free catalog from
New Directions, 80 Eighth Avenue, New York 10011   †Bilingue